American Dream

American Dream

Greed, Capitalism, and the Failure of Spirituality in America

A spiritual, inspirational, and motivational book
with a twist of humor

By Lillie Sandridge-Hill

iUniverse, Inc.
Bloomington

American Dream
Greed, Capitalism, and the Failure of Spirituality in America

Copyright © 2012 by Lillie Sandridge-Hill.

iUniverse books may be ordered through booksellers or by contacting:

iUniverse
1663 Liberty Drive
Bloomington, IN 47403
www.iuniverse.com
1-800-Authors (1-800-288-4677)

Because of the dynamic nature of the Internet, any web addresses or links contained in this book may have changed since publication and may no longer be valid. The views expressed in this work are solely those of the author and do not necessarily reflect the views of the publisher, and the publisher hereby disclaims any responsibility for them.

Any people depicted in stock imagery provided by Thinkstock are models, and such images are being used for illustrative purposes only. Certain stock imagery © Thinkstock.

ISBN: 978-1-4759-3022-1 (sc)
ISBN: 978-1-4759-3023-8 (ebk)

Printed in the United States of America

iUniverse rev. date: 06/20/2012

FOR WHOSOEVER SHALL CALL UPON THE
NAME OF THE LORD SHALL BE SAVED.
Romans 10:13

In memory of my mother and father

Contents

Introduction... xi

One - The American Greed... 1
Two - Pain 5
Three - Money 9
Four - Realization 13
Five - The Renewal 18
Six - The Test.. 22
Seven - Work in Progress 26
Eight - The Belief... 30
Nine - The Open Gates... 36
Ten - Homeward Bound 41
Eleven - The Journey 45
Twelve - Reflection.. 50
Thirteen - Meditative Visions....................................... 55
Fourteen - Words of Knowledge (Scripture)............... 66

Conclusion - Inspirational Food for Thought 75

Introduction

I have been told that greed is a state of mind and that all people are susceptible.

Greed, though it is condemned in the Bible, has created and doomed many empires. The Roman writer Horace said the more you acquire, the more you desire. When you have a fear of the future, more is never enough. Capitalism is the seed to excess, I have heard. It is said when capitalism began, greed would never be the same. You cannot serve two masters, and greed is the enemy of charity. The 1929 stock market crash was caused by a corrupt banking system. When the market crashed, it took everyone with it. Greed: is it the devil or in our DNA? Can we defeat it? These questions have been put before us. What do you think?

Remember, the wealthy are not going to give it back. The economic crisis, global warming, and apocalyptic visions are warning us of what is now knocking at the door. The end is near, they say, but my understanding is that no one knows the end: not the children, only the father. I hope my book will inspire, motivate, encourage you, and even humor you to live by these words of the wise. May God bless your journey.

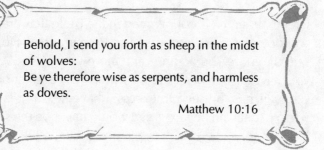

Behold, I send you forth as sheep in the midst of wolves:
Be ye therefore wise as serpents, and harmless as doves.

Matthew 10:16

One

The American Greed

The American greed did not begin to crumble in society when most of us suspected it did.

I suspect it started a long time ago, back when it went unnoticed, like a smoldering fire. Some things are not noticed until they are well upon us. My suspicions are that many hundreds of years ago, greed came upon America even before it was an empire, back when land was stolen, lives were expedient, and hardship was a way of life for the poor and middle class. As the years passed, those who flourished gave hope to those who had not yet accomplished the dream but saw it as something they could have if they worked hard and long, hoping their day would come soon. Some cheated, stole, schemed, and did whatever it took to get rich because they had no patience for the time it took to grow wise with the wealth that they wanted so badly. Still America grew and grew to a point where greed was noticed by only a few.

It has always amazed me how we are so blinded by our wants that we blot out just meeting our needs so that we can live a life that would extend blessings to others through sharing, fairness, and forgiveness. There is nothing wrong with wealth as long as it is not plundered through others' expense. To build an empire is hard work I'm sure, but as it is with all buildings, it must be built on a strong foundation. If not, as we all know, it will crumble because it is not very stable. Quick and fast gratification can keep the ball rolling toward that crumbling point. This country was built on capitalism (a.k.a. greed). Why else would the price of goods be so high when quality of workmanship is not as evident as you might think it should be. Life is a struggle if you are rich or poor. Love, faith, and the grace of God are the only differences that make it easier to have a life that is really worth living.

God created this world so that we could make decisions for ourselves and make our own future lives healthy, wealthy, and wise. We were given this chance; how we use it is our choice, for better or worse. We all know people who have made poor choices, but it is not too late to change things; it's not over yet. For those who care, changing is easy.

We can start being kind to others at any moment in our lives, not just on any special day. Caring people become less selfish when helping others. Selfishness is like hoarding one's love from other people and our environment. Some people hold on to things they think will bring them self-worth; those people only care about self-preservation. The only way to enlightenment is to see beyond yourself for the betterment of all life on earth. We should appreciate everyone's contribution because there is a reason for everything, even if we cannot see why.

Think of all the things that make you happy; are they awe-inspiring, or self-fulfilling, or just plain impressive? There is nothing wrong with elevating one's status in life. It's just that one grows strong on obtaining goods that will perish when he or she leaves this world instead of building impressive thing like love, charity, and faith, which will accompany him or her in eternal life. You can stand before God with no shame or regret in your heart. No matter what your goal is in life, nothing can flourish for the good without the grace of God's blessings. The most important things in life are not measured by our wants but by the needs of others. Jesus said whatever we do to each other we do to him. Is it not a good feeling to know that when you are being nice to someone, you are being nice to Jesus? We are here for each other, not just for ourselves. Look around at this beautiful planet we live on and all the different species. There seems to have been a plan in mind for our accomplishments to excel in a good way, so let's not destroy what was given to us by God.

The planet might have grown through capitalism, but it may not survive it. Remember the expression too big to fail? The foundation will never be stable, not until we build on solid values. We must stop our self-destruction and learn what history has taught us. For in the teachings of the past, we can build on a stronger foundation and still have hope for our future, and our children's future. Hope is a good thing; we must take it and use it in a manner befitting of what the Lord expected. Hopes and dreams are good; they keep the ball rolling for great improvement in society as a whole, not in the demise of others or the downfall of so many. I believe in free enterprise, just not at the expense of people's lives, especially to the point of greed.

Some people will walk over others to see their pockets full of cash and to say, "I got mine, you get yours." Greed, greed can ruin anything or anybody to the point of vivid destruction.

The need to have more than needed, to look bigger and better than most, is not a quality that you should present to God on your special day when you have your life reviewed before him and say, "Look what I did on earth, how rich and respected I was." That would not necessarily be a good thing to mention at this time. You must take measures in your present life to improve on your eternal life, and greed will not get you there. Nothing good ever comes from greed, so why do we do it? No one is perfect; we are all born into sin—everyone. Everything takes effort. It is the direction you take that effort in that matters. Here's a simple rule: If it is illegal, immoral, or unethical, don't do it. This is a simple enough rule, don't you think?

> So when they continued asking him, he lifted up himself, and said unto them, he that is without sin among you, let him first cast a stone at her.
>
> John 8:7

Two

Pain

The pain of any failure in life is not worthy of any condolences when it is self-inflicted. Pity not the fool who lives and does not learn, right? Wrong. There is always a lesson to learn from, but remember we are only human. We don't always learn at the same pace. Forgiveness and learning to move on is what helps us to grow stronger, and taking that strength in the right direction helps us to heal. You would think most life lessons would teach us to not repeat the same mistakes twice, but some of us take longer to see the pitfalls in life. Although some of us see, we are blinded by false hope or just too impatient to go the long and steady route. Pain is a true feeling of despair. It hurts a whole lot, no matter the cause. You would think good would always overcome evil, but not when greed is involved, for it is one of the seven deadly sins, and some people pursue it with a vengeance.

Some people think their everyday accomplishments are done on their own strength and ingenuity. Oh, the pain of finding out differently. God has offered a passageway that can help us through the good and bad days in life. It always amazes me to see the pain tolerance of some people. Have we become desensitized to pain? Has it become acceptable and tolerable? Is it mind over matter or the fear of failure to those that see failure and fear it? Whatever the case might be, nothing is more important than your eternal soul, for temptation is but a ploy to trip you up. God knows this, and this is why he sent his son. We are only human; we make mistakes. All you have to do is pick yourself up and dust yourself off, ask the Lord for forgiveness, and try to do better next time. Sincerity is always felt by the ones who care about you. To lead a wonderful life, do unto others as you would have them do unto you.

The journey you take in life is what you make of it. I know some people don't seem to get a fair shake even from the beginning, but remember everything has a purpose, even if we don't understand it. Things will be revealed to us in due time, just have patience, oh ye of little faith. Do you want to be part of the painful experience or start on the road to healing? We can take away some of the pain by facing the true meaning of the life that was planned for us or continue down the road of destruction until we meet our demise; the choice is ours. Being a good person is not good enough; we must act with hands on when helping others. Let's face it, if there was an easy way through life, I am sure someone would have figured it out by now. Pain is an attention getter, an acknowledgment of true discomfort. Why do some people seem to experience more pain than others? What comes easy for some may be hard for others.

Some people maneuver themselves well through life, and some have difficulty just getting up in the morning.

Life really is like a box of chocolates; you never know what you are going to get. You can make the best of what you get, though. When life get tough, the tough get going, right? Wrong. They get mad and then get tougher and then get going. A complete waste of energy, I think. Get stronger through prayer, and *then* get going. Now there are those that stop trying; they give up and move through life like a robot. Some just lay low. What is your pain level? Some people call pain motivation; some suffer from paralysis, some see it as a wake-up call. This world is going to change as we know it, and we have begun to feel the pain. Remember, think good thoughts, do good deeds, smile, and laugh a lot. Evil will take care of itself without our help. Anyway, who needs the pain?

We do not need to reinvent the wheel. Everything is already within our power; we just need to stop being greedy and selfish and causing a lot of pain to ourselves and others. The journey we take could be more meaningful and prosperous to us all if we did not let greed blindfold us. Our perspective sometimes leads us in a downhill spiral of pain and misery, which can be hard to climb out of. So look at life as an adventure, be mindful of others, and know some things will never be as we wish. Guide your life in the right direction, because in the second coming, everything will come to pass. We can take away some of the pain by facing the true meaning of life that was planned for us. We have the instructions given to us in the Bible. Remember, your life, your choice.

I said in mine heart, God shall judge the righteous and the wicked: for there is a time there for every purpose and for every Work.

Ecclesiates 3:17

Three

Money

Money circulates throughout the world as a universal language of status for those who have it. This can be a downfall for some and a lifestyle for others. The love of money is the root of evil when it leads you to greed; selfishness can grow inside your heart and mind, taking away any sense of reasoning that will help you to prosper and become a charitable human being. Basic instincts give way to survival of the fittest, causing some people to ignore the needs of others for their own desires for success. When we weave threads of deceit into our daily lives to make money, deception can spiral out of control. When we honor the glory of God for blessing us, the path is straight and narrow.

Money can become a part of the way you live your life; it can keep your judgment cloudy. Keeping your head clear and your heart free of deceit will help in those times when life throws a stumbling block in the middle of the road and you just want things to work out without feeling stressed and tangled up in life's many episodes of pending whatevers. Money has always been an issue for some people, especially if they make it a top priority; it is the only language some people will listen too. I'm sure you have heard of the haves and have-nots. The haves are the people that sway your life in the direction of helping the have-nots, or giving the haves more power to control you (secretly, of course). Sometimes you cannot tell when you are being sucked in by capitalism, if you are enjoying the trip. Life is grand only when you have a grasp on it, and only God can give you that peace; everything else is fleeting.

When I was growing up in the fifties, life appeared simple enough. Money grew on trees, in my mind's eye. You could buy a lot for a quarter, which did not seem difficult to get (unless I had to ask my father for it; then it seemed as if I had to fill out a credit application to get it, because he always asked what did I need it for). Money, how great thou are in determining the importance of someone's life expectancy, by human standards anyway. As I grew older, I saw money as only a tool and nothing else, and I do mean nothing else. You should not let money determine your self-worth in this world. Life is of greater importance to mankind and what God expects of us. Money has sent many people into ruins and helped many others to prosper. Money should be dealt with like any tool, and that is with careful usage and not blind ambition.

Money and greed can go hand in hand; a lot is not enough in the eyes of some. How you determine your own self-worth is up to you; just remember we should put our trust in God. There is nothing wrong with being blessed in life, but you may notice the changes it brings about in a person's life are not always great. Jesus said it is easier for a camel to go through the eye of a needle than for a rich man to get into heaven. We always want more and more things that do not make us a better person, just a person with more things. When we challenge ourselves in a more positive way of living, like being kind and charitable to others, life feels good and things feel right in the world.

When we wake up in the morning, we should have a zest for life itself, not another grind to obtain riches beyond our needs. Life really is good when you put God first and not money.

What do you think would happen if we went back to bartering instead of using money to obtain goods? I think we would probably have only what we need in life. What we really need is faith in God; this world is not the promised land, or the land of milk and honey, just the stepping stone to the true land of bliss and harmony we call heaven. There are no shortcuts in life; we all have to go through some test to be worthy of being in the eternal presence of God's love. Never lose faith in him that gives life. Money cannot buy God's love; he does not need anything we have, since he is the one who has given us the things we do have in life. When we look back on our lives, from time to time we may notice certain patterns as we walk on this earth. That pattern can show God the type of person we really are, and as always he can see into our heart, he knows our intentions for living as he would want us to.

Do not get me wrong; money can be a good thing. It can help you help others and help yourself in different ways to sustain life. Money can also be a tricky tool to use; try not to let it overpower your sense of direction. Common sense is a good accessory to wear with money. Taking steps to be aware in your daily decisions can help you stay on the path of righteousness in a world corrupted with greed. How we live our lives can make a difference in someone else's life, and when we think of others first, we don't seem to have a drive for the love of money. The invention of money must have seemed like a great accomplishment thousands of years ago, not knowing it would separate so many people from each other; was this the first sign of greed? Our accomplishments should always reflect our values in life; this is our legacy.

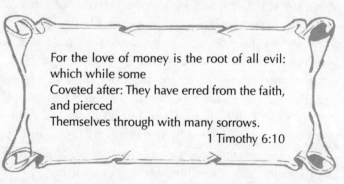

For the love of money is the root of all evil: which while some
Coveted after: They have erred from the faith, and pierced
Themselves through with many sorrows.

1 Timothy 6:10

Four

Realization

Realization is something that can open your eyes to help you see a clearer picture of what is going on in your life. Too bad it has to slap some of us in the face before we can see it. "Smile, God loves you." When you wake up in the morning, what is the first thing you realize? I'm alive, time to start a new day. Every day you live, you have the opportunity to start fresh. It's like getting a second chance every time you wake up. I personally like getting a second chance every day I live. You know the old expression, "If I had died yesterday, I would not have learned that today." Please see every day as an opportunity to progress and not regress. Sometimes, realization can be shocking and very upsetting. Some people do not handle this well, so we should not ignore a time bomb ticking, don't you think? Tick, tick, tick; please move as far away as you can from the ticking sound, people. This has "Professional help needed" written all over it.

The warning signs we get in life should not be ignored. Living in the same world as everyone else does not mean there is cohesion in values. Sometimes, people only see their wants, even if they are hazardous to their health or well-being. Quick and fast gratification or just plain old too scared to venture out from the things that are so wrong in this world; the world scares a lot of people who like to follow the in crowd and not think of the end results. Everyone has a choice in the way they live, except the weak ones, who depend upon the mercy and kindness of others. I know it is hard to get through life without tripping up from time to time. Jesus' crucifixion gave us the chance to renew with hope every day that we are given to live on this earth and do the best we can toward each other. I do not believe God meant for us to be a draconian society of people, but he does expect obedience to his word.

Here is a quote from Mary Catherine Bateson: "We are not what we know but what we are willing to learn." Life is what you make it, and people can make it hard, evil, or nice. It is all in one's perspective on how to live in this world. Make sound choices on how you live, for your eternal life does depend on it. The rules and roles in life are not always clear; they can be confusing when you look at people in groups and categorized sections.

One thing is always clear and consistent: the Bible. Read it and learn everything you need to know about life. This book has all the answers to any questions you might have. This book will not lie to you or lead you in the wrong direction. We always have a choice.

I have always been resistant against putting people into molds and telling them this is the way it should be; we should follow our heavenly father's advice; we will be better off.

Deny Jesus now, and he will deny knowledge of you later before the father. Realization is yours, people, just embrace it as you would a loved one. Realization will lead us to the new American dream. This dream can give us a better quality of life for our children. When things are dealt with truthfully, we cannot cry wolf as if we were expecting a less threatening solution to the problems we have gotten ourselves into. We should stop living frivolously if we expect better outcomes with our daily life. Making decisions that will sustain you will take effort and time, so get ready for more self-awareness of what you are doing before you do it. Spending less and saving more will not hinder the growth of America; it will give our country a better perspective in the direction we should be going with clarity and understanding of what God wants for us. When making any decision, first consider the outcome, or are we a bunch of five-year-olds needing our hands to be held?

People sometimes let others lead them into uncharted waters. There is nothing wrong with getting expert advice, but remember the final decision is yours, so when you get that funny feeling in the bottom of your stomach, go with your first thought. Common sense will not fail you. This is a safety net that we have to use for rationalization of a situation. I know what you are thinking, some people are not born with common sense, and if they are, they ignore it. Just because some people have the tools doesn't mean they will use them. Remember, you can lead a horse to water but you can't make him drink. Realization is a personal journey we each have to take individually to make sense of life. When you are informed about a situation, you will make better decisions. When we listen, we learn.

Realization can be painful, so just do it; renewal is what's next, and having a rush of energy will overcome the pain in a nonnarcotic way and leave you with a clearer mind. Realize it is what it is; you can take the bull by the horns so to speak and make your life easier day to day. Since all people are not like minded, expect some ups and downs in daily encounters, and get over it; that's life. Take time to stop and notice the beauty of the land we live in and the ever changing landscape that keeps us moving. Things are always changing and will always be changing in a way; you either adapt to it or get swallowed up by it, your choice. When we make the decision to change for a better life, we will be able to breathe a sigh of relief from our daily decision making. Beauty is in the realization, and realization is beautiful.

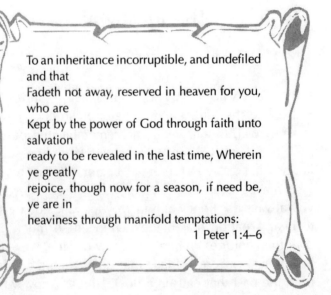

To an inheritance incorruptible, and undefiled and that
Fadeth not away, reserved in heaven for you, who are
Kept by the power of God through faith unto salvation
ready to be revealed in the last time, Wherein ye greatly
rejoice, though now for a season, if need be, ye are in
heaviness through manifold temptations:

1 Peter 1:4–6

Five

The Renewal

I like renewal; it's when you blossom and grow. I also like the innocence of being fresh and new. In this renewal, though, you can remember the past, so your fresh start will be with knowledge, because you know what got you there. All beginnings are hard at first, maybe even painful, but you will get passed it; you always do. Renewal and growth walk side by side to heal a nation that has experienced so much pain over the centuries. When we renew our life, we start a beginning with fresh ideas that don't mimic anything from the past that caused a downfall; we know where we went wrong. Remember greed. Do not forget the past, and you have a greater chance of not repeating it unless you like pain. Some people do like pain; for some reason, it is the only thing that makes them feel alive. Go figure. Life is what you make it. So we will renew and have a new start because of the teachings of Jesus Christ, and this gives us the strength we need to carry on.

Renewal begins with each new day. One day at a time, we are led in the direction of hopes and dreams of a future that leads to a renewal of the heart, soul, and mind. We have the chance to start over every day we are alive and to change our perspectives for a better life. Each day can bring a freshness in the way we deal with things. Sure, starting anew can be painful; life is a mixture of ups and downs. That's how we grow stronger and gain strength. God has made us to survive the seasons of life and endure hardships so that we may grow strong with each storm. Anyone can falter; all living organisms replenish, renew, or restart.

We have always had the drive to push forward, even when we did not do the right things to get us there. Renewal will help us with this and bring in a new way of thinking for those who do not want to repeat past mistakes.

All we ever needed was what we already had before our eyes, but if not for the blindfold called greed, we could have seen what we were taught, and that is the teachings of Jesus, who died on the cross to save us. Can we not take just a moment before we speak or do things that will lead us into the oblivion of deep, dark despair? Life is not a bowl of cherries or a bowl of anything. The cold, hard fact is that each person's life is full of hard, funny, eye opening, cruel, ongoing, boring, lovely, and kind emotions. When we gather our strength, only then can we renew. You literally have to regroup every day to be able to stay in the running, or else you will fall behind. This is where you really need the help of the almighty.

Face it, we cannot live without the grace of God. Those who try will always meet their demise with any of their endeavors. The truth has been laid before us. Take this knowledge and grow in health and well-being, and life will look at you with eyes of renewal and freshnes.

Nothing is promised to us but our salvation, if we just believe in him and trust in his teachings. This is part of the renewal process. Each and every day, you will feel a calmness come over you. You will be able to deal with minor annoyances that can be easily brushed away; you can deal with bigger problems systematically without losing your sanity. When you have done your best, it is best to move on and not dwell in the house of pain. The renewal process must go on for the survival of your well-being. The passage of time will heal a lot of misfortunes. In time, things will come together in peace and harmony in your mind and spirit, which will be with you all the days of your life. You cannot expect different results with the same old plan, day in and day out. This is the definition of insanity. Only when we become desensitized can we start to want more and more stuff to dull the pain of what we feel as being inadequate. All the things that were supposed to make our life easier have actually caused more debt, more stress, and not enough time to enjoy these things as we would like.

Growth awaits us. No one is perfect, and we all get tired. So keep on keeping on until you feel the love, because that is your ticket to salvation and the life beyond any happiness you could ever imagine here on earth. Renewal is the key. To share in happiness, love, peace, and well-being with others, you have to display these qualities yourself, not a dog-eat-dog mentality. We should love everyone, not for their qualities, but because they are human just like you are. I know they may not appear human, but it is a life, and God will deal with the rest later. It is easier to care for someone you love; try caring for someone you do not know. Now that is an accomplishment. Do unto others as you would have them do unto you, and you will not go wrong. This is the easiest path to renewal and the simplest way to start each day in harmony with others. God bless the renewal process, for this is the beginning of our new life.

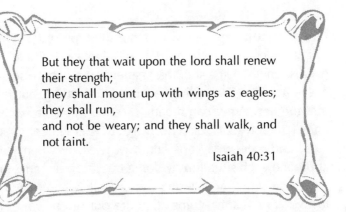

But they that wait upon the lord shall renew their strength;
They shall mount up with wings as eagles; they shall run,
and not be weary; and they shall walk, and not faint.

Isaiah 40:31

Six

The Test

Oh my, a test, you say. This is not the type of test you might expect. This is not a test of talent or aptitude or even strength. Just a short assessment on a 0 to 10 scale to see how you are feeling so far on our healing journey into the new American dream; 0 represents no anxiety, and 10 represents extreme anxiety. Remember, you can handle everyday ups and downs easily when you approach each situation by doing the best you can with what you know and letting the rest fall where it may, for we cannot solve things that are out of our control. So stop letting yourself get all anxious about things you cannot control. Anyway, God will handle it, and you won't even have to get your hands dirty. Prayer is a good thing to keep in store also. If you can do this, you have passed the test; if not try, try again until you succeed. Practice makes perfect, you know. Just take a long deep breath and let it go.

This part of the journey is a short trip. Misery loves company, and we do not indulge such notions that will eat away at the fabric of our souls. Life is short when you are looking down the barrel of gloom and despair. Smile and be happy, stop and smell the roses (unless you are allergic), and take some time for yourself. Whatever your situation is, it will only last as long as you want it to. When you stop feeling sorry for yourself, dry your tears and ask God for help. All any child of God has to do is ask to receive. He will never close a door on you without opening another. Ye of so little faith, he will bring you through it. None of us know what is next; we cannot see the future, and if we could, would you want to? Would you take advice that could help you have a better future or go bury your head in the sand? All we need to know is what we know already, which is written in the Bible; this is our salvation that will lead us straight to the gates of heaven.

Life is good; we are the ones who fail to instill moral, ethical, and legal living into our lifestyles. I know some people will never learn, never listen. What can you do if these people know the facts but continue on as if they don't care? Move on and away from those who will drag you down, but always pray for them. The blindfold does not come off at the same time for everyone. There will be many tests in your lifetime that test your judgment on the right things to do; some people can't seem to grasp this concept of honesty. It seems to evade them. Life can be difficult at times; why make it more complicated with dishonesty to yourself and others? You know it's going to come back and bite you in the butt. Avoid the lie now, and have no regrets tomorrow. You know the expression "Pay now or pay later." The inevitable will happen; it's just Murphy's law.

When we are being tested on something, we get nervous, even when we know the answers like the back of our hand. For some reason or another, we think there is going to be a trick question just to see if we are paying attention. So look out because sometimes there are trick questions, not to trip you up, but to see if you are paying attention. When life comes crashing down, do you feel like you are being tested or being picked on, or just maybe you're the unluckiest person in the world? Get a grip; life happens, and it happens to all of us in some form or fashion. What bothers me is when it happens to an innocent; you know, the ones who cannot not take care of themselves without help, like children, the elderly, and the disabled. My only comforting thought is there will come a day when judgment will reign over the lawless, and they will be punished for their iniquities. The lost ones will be restored by the grace of God to an everlasting peace of no more tears.

When we are being tested, take heart in knowing that the test is just to see how we are getting along and our knowledge of life thus far in our journey. This is not a pass or fail grade as in school, but to see how you are holding up; you might need a little help in going in the right direction. Some people do not believe in testing, but remember Job was tested severely and he pulled through, without any help from his friends. Just have faith and believe that Jesus died for our salvation; believe in his teachings, and trust in his words. I once read that it would be better to believe there is a God and die and find out there wasn't, than to believe there is no God and die and find out there was. I think without God's presence, we would not live on such a beautiful planet and have the choices we have. Left up to our own devices, we would not have gotten so far without some intervention.

> And I was with you in weakness, and in fear, and in much trembling.
> And my speech and my preaching was not with enticing words of man's
> Wisdom, but in demonstration of the spirit and of power; That your faith
> Should not stand in the wisdom of men, but in the power of God.
>
> 1 Corinthians 2:3–5

Seven

Work in Progress

When we start any project in life, there are many kinks to work out. The hurdles in the beginning can seem treacherous, and there are no simple and fast answers here. Listening and talking with others sometimes can make things more confusing, especially when their ideas are not Christian based. The process of growth does not always give us the end product we hope for. The one power we do have is to change things as we know it, which people have done for ages. Nothing new, just more hard work, but hard work is what has built this country. Let's not be afraid of a future that can instill hope in so many people again. When any one person moves in the right direction, it has a trickle-down effect on others. This is a good example of why we need to consider more than ourselves when we make a decision, because no one lives on earth truly alone. No matter what direction you move in, you affect someone else in this world. Life will always be what we make of it. The only promise that we have is from God.

When you believe in something, life takes a different path than it does without belief. Belief is a strong sense of understanding things as we comprehend them to be. When you believe in capitalism, it puts a different perspective on the way you deal with life in general. Materialism seems to be a greater factor in our decisions, even when we do not acknowledge it to be. If we are to turn this country around for us and future generations, we have got to go back to the teachings of Jesus. When you read the words that Jesus taught to his disciples and others who gathered to listen to him, there is no greed, no malice, no misleading words to confuse you or make you believe in something that is not true. Progress can only begin when we believe in the word and not base our lives on how much we can obtain in material possessions. Material things are good only to the extent of self-gratification and the belief that people will love you more; without possessions, people can only love you for yourself, which is the way it should be.

Look around you and see the beautiful, amazing things living on this planet; you can see the vision God has for us, not the picture that Satan has painted in our minds to corrupt us and make us servants of all that is wrong in this world. The true discipline of brotherhood among us will help us gain back an understanding of our purpose here on earth. Remember, we always have a choice in the matters of this world. You cannot hide anything, so believe in what is right and strive only to obtain God's blessings to maintain a better quality of life. Even when you are weak and do not have the strength to carry on, he knows your heart. Life is hard, no doubt about it, but your struggles can be eased when you believe in Christ and you can see your progress in each passing day. Each day that you live is another chance to progress and improve your surroundings. Only the greedy and self-serving seek to please only themselves without thinking of others in this world.

Progress as we know is not an overnight accomplishment; the rewards don't just show up when the morning comes. A work in progress is just that: work. Tackling large issues can bring gratification in the long run. Dealing with ups and downs in life is what makes us human in working with other people; we need to understand the needs of other people, needs which are not unlike our own. When we go through life spending only time and money on ourselves, we will become selfish in so many ways. These people look to get, not give to others. Some people cannot see the cliff they are about to walk off. Having a blindfold on will hinder you from moving forward and progressing the way God wants you to. Moving forward is something we can do in light of the past. We are human, and every day we live, we have the chance to progress, not regress. When making decisions, do you think what would Jesus do? Most of us don't; maybe we should.

For things to progress in life, they need to be extended in the right direction at the right time with the best intentions; anything less will not survive the test of time. There is a season for everything that is bound by the goodness of our lord and savior. Moving in a forward direction does not promise us anything other than a forward motion. The belief in God is what propels the motion in the right direction with the best results. Anytime you go against the grain, you take the chance of a painful abrasion. A work in progress is an ongoing process of the mind, body, and spirit; a lifetime of work will culminate when you review your deeds. Not all will be good, because no one is perfect, but showing love to others will show God that you love him. When you start your day, start it with the intention of being someone that you would want to be around, and follow in the footsteps of a person who believes in progress for all.

How can a life in progress help mankind? It will show strong responsibility for all who wish to live with God's blessings and do unto others; by showing love and compassion, we can live on a planet that will restore hope to the lost and faith to the faithless. To turn things around is not a big task, just think less is more. Stop trying to impress those that cannot get past their own iniquities in this world, much less help you with yours. You feel good when you do good things for others. A work in progress takes a long time; impatient people want quick gratification, but it is a short journey for those who believe the work in progress will always be ongoing and rewarding in the long run.

> And we know that all things work together for
> good to them that love God,
> to them who are the called
> according to his purpose.
>
> Romans 8:28

Eight

The Belief

A strong belief in capitalism can become twisted and complicated after years of believing this is the best way to go. The progress we have made in life is based on our belief system, and to change our way of thinking at this point will bring about a hard and long change in the American way of life. People with a materialistic mind-set will definitely resist the most. Growing up in a society of haves and have-nots has a tendency to make some people believe the only way to happiness is money. True, money pays the bills, but does it keep you on the road to a successful life with your fellow man? No, it does nothing that will bring prosperity to the needy on a regular basis, it just prolongs the inevitable outcome. Most of the problems we have in this world do not come from being poor, but from being overcrowded, destroying the environment, and mistreating each other. All of these things can be fixed without money, but with common sense on a daily basis. I believe this planet has everything we need if we use it properly and treat it well. We do not need big houses or big cars; we do

30

not need five or more of the same thing. What we need is to discipline our behavior. Some people are bent on impressing others, as if that will make you a better person. In the eyes of God, we are all his children, so if you want to impress someone, impress him; he holds your eternal life in his hands, which will truly determine your outcome in this world.

Our current belief system makes things more attainable in life, with capitalism at the head of the table. Capitalism promotes motivation, which is not always in tune with the well-being of the weak; only the strong will survive such scrutiny. When you believe in something so strongly that it pushes you to the edge of financial ruin, then and only then can you wake up and face reality. Sure, there were institutions that led us in the wrong direction, but they did not put a gun to our head. We went in greed, people, face it. Some people will repeat history, but other will remember and not repeat it. God lets us choose the direction we go in. We need to start making better choices and stop playing the blame game. Always wake up with good intentions; no matter how many times things go in the opposite direction, continue to do the best you can with what you have to work with. Any efforts you make in life will not go unnoticed by the most important one of all: God.

When I was a little girl, I believed that the number three was a good number for me. Having three of something made me happy: to have something in use, and something next in line, then something on the side just in case, so I would always have enough. Where I got this insecurity from, I do not know. Looking back on it now, it seems slightly odd to me, because that number did not guarantee anything. Everything you have can be destroyed at once, so this number can be irrelevant. Where we should put our most important belief in has nothing to do with materialism, but God, who gives us all we need and have in life. Maybe if we changed our belief system, we could change the way we live and treat others in our everyday life. Remembering the past, but always looking forward, will help us to move in the direction of hope and prosperity again in America, without the stain of greed to cloud our judgment in making good decisions. Trust in God and listen to his words; this will help in any choices you choose to make.

When our belief system takes us off the path of wisdom and leads us down the road to destruction, we should rethink our plans. Some people plan well, no matter what the economy is doing, and I believe that is because they do not get wrapped up in materialistic things beyond their needs. Some do not just flash the cash, but they flash the wealth to impress others, still not a good thing. Everything that goes up, can and will eventually come down. Trying to impress others is a weakness in ourselves. Why this is so important to people, I do not know, considering people cannot help you get to the most important destination you need to be going to. Doing things from the heart is what will impress God, the one who really matters and who can grant you an eternal life of heavenly bliss. Do things from the heart, and let the ones who only care about you when you are doing great, when you are rich and famous, slide down the rabbit hole and disappear. They will not be there when you need them anyways, only the ones who truly love you will stick by your side.

When you stop to evaluate your life and the people in it, do you feel happy and complete? Do you feel blessed to have people who love you for yourself in your life? One of the most important things to have in life is love. You can throw money at a person all day long and not improve their quality of life or make them feel like a child of God without love. I guess that's why a rich person can be lonely even with lots of money in the bank. The belief that money will solve your problems has a long history of disappointment for many. Yet we strive for the almighty dollar, which is only good when used properly, but most people will abuse it if they have half the chance and end up back where they started. Now those who do not abuse money but use it wisely may still honor their riches more than they honor God. Bless the child that has his own, but think wisely and pray for wisdom in using what God has blessed you with.

Changing the way you feel about money does not change the need for it, but it will put things in a better perspective when spending it for the things you need and want to have, considering you have worked for it. Money is only the root of evil when we worship it. There were many people of wealth in the Bible whom God loved very much, and that is because he came first in their life; their life was blessed with wealth of all sorts. Remember that God gave you the knowledge, strength, and ability to earn money; nothing is obtained without him. The lord giveth and he can also taketh. When we grew up in this world, we were not always taught the true fundamentals of money, only to earn it, save some, spend some, be charitable with some, but never to be thankful for the ability to have some and thank the lord for blessing us with it, for it is not always a given for all. There were many who fell from grace because of greed, only to ponder where they went wrong and not learn from their own demise or blame others because greed blinded them from the reality of spending beyond their means.

God wants us to believe in him and his teachings so that we may live a prosperous life. All things were made by God; nothing is possible without him. Your beliefs should be based on the words of our lord and savior, and not from worldly concepts of what is wrong or right in this world. There is nothing in the Bible that will lead you down the road of despair if you follow it. Life can take you far and wide on a path of enlightenment, or it can take you on a perilous journey. The beliefs you have in life can make you or break you; it is your choice. People who have not been around for long may not see a pattern that can lead to a road with a fork in it. The path is straight and narrow for only so long, then we get to the point where we need to acknowledge our behavior. Wisdom is a great thing for those who obtain it and a sad ending for those who never reach it in life.

Because thou sayest, I am rich, and increased with goods, and have
need of nothing; and knowest not that thou art wretched, and
miserable, and poor, and blind, and naked:

Revelation 3:17

Nine

The Open Gates

Now that the gates are opened (and I do mean gates, because you will go through many in your lifetime), see how long you can stay on the straight and narrow; challenge yourself to see how well you can be a part of the solution and not the problem as you approach each fork in the road. Jesus said, "Enter ye at the straight gate: for wide is the gate, and broad is the way that leadeth to destruction, and many there be which go in thereat. Because straight is the gate, and narrow is the way, which leadeth unto life, and few there be that find it. (Matthew 7:13-14). To be honest with you, when I first started to write about the American dream and all the greed supported by capitalism and the lack of spirituality in America, it was just an analogy that gave me a voice in what was going on in the world. I am now beginning to understand not only how we got here, but how we can get to a point of resolution. I hope my words have a revitalizing effect on how you view your life and the future of others.

The gates are opened for all who go through them. Just stay on the path; the light will lead the way. Darkness only comes when you stray. We should live our lives to be a blessing to others. The gates are opened to lead us on a journey in the direction of peace and harmony. Only when you venture off the path do you encounter a world of destructive behavior. Some people wake up every morning mad at the world and attempt to bring you down with them. Do not, I repeat, do not let these people suck the life out of you; stay on the path of righteousness and you will be blessed by your perseverance. I know it can be hard at times, but pray for them and pray for yourself, and your spirit will be lifted, and your thoughts will be yours again very soon. When you pray, your path is cleared of debris that can make you stumble. Happiness is in the truth, and despair lies within the falsehood of the deceitful.

God so loved the world that he gave his only begotten son so that we may be saved. So keep trying, and your efforts will not go unnoticed; your life will thank you for making good choices. Think positive; it will help your state of mind if things do not work out the way you want, and it will help you to keep going forward one day at a time. This reminds me of one of my mother's favorite songs, "One Day at a Time." "One day at a time," she would sing, "one day at a time, sweet Jesus, that's all I ask of thee." I remember this song and knew it was one of my mother's favorites, so I had the choir sing it at her funeral. The lead singer in the choir sang the song so beautifully that it still brings tears to my eyes when I hear her singing it in my mind some twenty-eight years later. Now this song is one of my favorites too.

This song and "Amazing Grace" are my favorite Christian songs. I wish I could carry a tune because I know at least these two songs would be on my lips all the time, especially in this day and age. I do not think many people know about the man who wrote "Amazing Grace" or what gave him the words of wisdom to write it. John Newton was a slave ship captain who changed his ways and eventually became a minister. One stormy trip was all it took to open his eyes: "I was blind but now I see." I will probably never know why it sometimes takes a disaster before we "see." What I do know is it is better late than never. It is always the darkest before the dawn, my mother would say. She had many little quips like this for life's little moments, and I am grateful for every one I heard her say, even though at the time I did not understand many of them. After I had lived a little myself and experienced life's ups and downs, her words kept ringing in my ears, and then I did understand.

Make good use of your time while you have the time. Try not to spin your wheels in a way that will hurt yourself and others, which can cause a chain reaction that will bring harm to all. The collapse of the American dream is not a metaphor for the disaster of humankind; it is just my conclusion that we need to get our act together now! The longer you live in the land of the lost, the harder it is to find your way homeward bound. My father was a great force in helping me to learn to forgive others; maybe he felt the need to be forgiven, as we all do sometimes. My children and grandchildren have given me the love and respect that I need along life's journey, and this comes from a place that money

cannot buy. I am grateful for my life with my family and thank God for every moment he gives me to be a better person. The gates are open; let us travel in the right direction and try to not get lost on the trip home.

The ways of the world can be a stumbling block for some, because who does not want to fit in and be welcomed? When we change our values to fit in, then there's a problem. The seven deadly sins are not mentioned in the Bible, but they can lead to ruin for those who partake in them: pride, greed, envy, anger, lust, gluttony, and sloth. If any of these things are picking away at your life, get rid of them now before it is too late. These things can be a stumbling block to a life of prosperity, tranquility, love, and harmony. The life we live will be reflected here on earth and how we will be remembered by others. It is your legacy that you leave behind you that will show God what type of person you were. Remember, every day is a new day for you to improve your daily deeds to yourself and mankind.

Know ye that the Lord he is God: it is he that hath made us, and not we ourselves; we are his people, and the sheep of his pastures. Enter into his gates with thanksgiving, and into his courts with praise: be thankful unto him, and bless his name. For the Lord is good; his mercy is everlasting; and his truth Endureth to all generations

Psalm 100:3–5

Ten

Homeward Bound

Now that you can see clearly in the direction you should be going, how does it make you feel? Some will make the journey home, and some will not make it completely through. Murphy's law, I guess, or maybe the route you take. Life will always be about choices, and there will always be obstacles in your path, like the seven deadly sins, that will pop up from time to time to test your love for worldly things. You should show your love for God, who sent his only begotten son to save us, for without him, you would never be able to be good enough to save yourself. We should make choices that show our obedience to God. We show obedience to many things that should not be the guiding light in our lives, things that will not give us eternal love, peace, or happiness, just a fleeting moment of satisfaction that will surely fade, leaving us hurt and broken. God has presented us with a lot of good things to choose from in our life, so choose wisely. Think, what would Jesus do in these situations?

There are many modes of transportation to take on your journey homeward bound; choose wisely, for you cannot travel backward to right the wrong you have caused, but you can be forgiven if you ask and believe in the one who died for your sins in this world. We all make mistakes, even the best of the best of us; no one is perfect. Making your trip home should be a learning experience; that's how we grow stronger and better. Some people do not just make mistakes, they make horrendous assaults against other people. Their evilness transcends any hope or mercy for them who choose the way of Satan over God's way to live. There is a hell, like there is a heaven. Where is your home? Your journey should reflect the path you are taking to get there, because we are all going home one day. Time is on no one's side. Time here on earth is not an illusion of the mind, but a reckoning of occurrences that we deal with on a daily basis; which leads us to a place where time does not exist as we know it. People who have had near-death experiences state there is no concept of time when they are in this state, for there is no need for time when you are experiencing an existence where there is no beginning or ending.

Going home is a journey you make, not a destination you strive for. You get there when you get there. Expediting the time does not work. You cannot stop the journey just because you are tired of the way things are going in your life. We all get weary from time to time. The journey is short for some and long for others. In the book of life, we each have our own path to follow, and no one knows how long we have to make the trip; some do not even get to make the trip before life is over for them. Whatever the case might be, each journey has its own length of time that can only be determined by the choices we make. We have to make many choices on the journey; it is the biggest trip we will ever make in life. Jesus did not promise us it would be easy, just very rewarding if we make it through. The journey is hard at times; that is why you should pray for guidance before venturing out on an endeavor. Ask for the blessing of God to guide you and keep you safe. Prayer works when you truly believe and live your life accordingly. Making decisions in life is the most difficult when you have the mind-set of worldly desires instead of the desires of the heavenly father, which will keep you in the light. You can deal with things better when you dwell in the house of the Lord.

How well we travel depends on how well prepared we are for the trip. I knew a woman once who would take a trip at the drop of a hat, with only a dollar in her pocket and a credit card, nothing much more than that. I always thought she was brave and daring. I wished that I could be brave like that also, but now I see it as living carelessly with no regard to "what if." There are always what ifs around each corner, whether you acknowledge them or not. No venture should be taken with little thought in mind to the consequences. Only the young can live as if they will live forever; age will eventually let you see your time on earth as being more valuable to you and everyone in your life who loves you, including God. As we journey in life, we see the pitfalls of trusting in the precarious way of life and start to wise up to the truth of the matter. Hopefully, we will learn things before it is too late to turn around and start in the direction that will get us to a point of calmness in our mind and soul, where we can see the light at the end of the tunnel.

In our homeward bound journey, we must stay tuned to the direction we go in. This trip can be long or short, but each step can keep you going in the right direction or take you off the path of enlightenment. Evaluate yourself from time to time and see if a life review will have you shaking in your boots; are you feeling like you were a very caring and understanding person while living among others? No one is perfect, but you can always make an attempt to do your best and not be selfish when dealing with others. Look around you; it is now 2012, the year that is supposed to end life as we know it on earth. We have already been saved; we just need to believe in Jesus. We should pray and trust in him to guide us in our daily life; he is our salvation. We do not need any other assurance. When you see people on television talking about the economy and the government, you can pretty much see the side they are on, whether it is for the rich, middle class, or poor. Even the religious leaders have a biased opinion. If we put God first, it would solve a multitude of problems and relieve of us of the bickering.

> Thy word is a lamp unto my feet, and a light unto my path.
>
> Psalm 119:105

Eleven

The Journey

You are now on your journey, with the light of God guiding your steps in a positive direction. I know it will take a long time before we are all on the same page, a very long time. So let's get started; it will be fun. Back to the basics of loving, caring, and sharing; it is not a hard thing to comprehend when greed and selfishness is not in the picture. The journey is what we need to bring us together as a people. I know some people will not make the journey, and I hate the thought of leaving them behind, but we can only make choices for ourselves; everyone must make their own choice. Remember the man who asked Jesus how he could follow him, and Jesus said to sell all his belongings. Jesus knew he was rich with worldly things. So you can imagine the look on this man's face, and as you know, he did not make the journey as one of Jesus' disciples. Some people have good intentions, but they have no desire to let some of their material world go. I think Job is a good example of a patient man; when he lost it all, he did not give up his trust in the Lord. We do not have to wait until we are dead to be blessed, just put the Lord first.

The journey is yours, and the time is yours; you only need to make the best of what is given to you in this world. We all make choices every day that will determine our true goal in this life. Just let the choices you make be something you can be proud of, not just for yourself, but for others also, since we live on the same planet, and what one person does can affect another. This is not the type of journey you can take over again in case you miss something the first time. You can do your best now by believing in the one who put you on this journey. Do unto others as you would have them do unto you. This is not a hard concept, but some people never grasp it on their journey through this world. Some people believe in reincarnation. What good is it to get a second chance if you do not remember the first chance you got? I do not remember a first journey, so to believe in Jesus as my Lord and savior now is something I can grasp and trust in, not a previous life that I cannot remember. Not to repeat a mistake is to remember the mistake made in the first place in order to learn from it.

Each person has their own journey to take in this world, their own calling to follow. We all have a choice in the direction we go, but we should not judge others as if we have always made the best decisions ourselves. What we can do is help each other by coming together and understanding what our true purpose is here on earth, and that is to help each other. God will not just speak to those who were the richest, most beautiful, or smartest on earth; this will not determine who will join him. As a matter of fact, this could be a disadvantage if you did not use this gift for the good of others. When we take the journey that will lead us to God, all hope on earth is magnified with a light of brilliance that will glow so brightly that we all can bask in his glory. Satan has led us down a path where we think bad is good and good is bad, if you want to survive in this world. Satan's trickery is not convincing to the ones who have been hurt by his lies and deceptions.

The world has to change as we know it; because of the damage done, we need to reverse some things at this point and change our lifestyle if we want the future generations to inherit a better place to live. The whole world is in turmoil and needs a readjustment to live according to what is best for people, not what is best for the ones who defy God's law. When God's law is obeyed, only the wicked seem to cry out for blood. No one has ever been hurt by a good and decent lifestyle. Since we cannot live on separate lands, then we will have to be our own steward of what actions we take in our daily lives and not be influenced by the world that perceives the seven deadly sins as a way of life. Not to worry, God will not forsake those who believe in him, and those will be the ones who have persevered and waited on his second coming. Their journey is perceived as the truth in their own eyes. Each person can only see what their mind will let them see. They need no glasses to see clearer. The wicked person perception is blocked by a blindfold that covers their eyes and will not be lifted until they start to believe in the word.

If people cannot see how going down the wrong path has demolished our well-being and brought this country to a weakened state, then they are the ones who will always blame others for their demise. They need to face the fact that each person takes their own journey and can be part of the problem when they make decisions that are greed based and have nothing to do with the well-being of others. As each person takes their journey in life, the path that they follow is their own. The choices you make, to go or stay, or sit or run, or cry or laugh, are your own, and this alone determines what happens next. Being at the right place at the wrong time is not a product of God, but Satan. We must understand that the journey we take is not promised as a smooth ride, and so things will not appear fair when Satan has a hand in the world. Stay true to God and you will be blessed with more than you could ever imagine. Remember, Job got it all back and then some.

And God shall wipe away all tears from their eyes; and There shall be no more death, neither sorrow, nor crying, neither shall there be any more pain: for the former things Are passed away. And he that sat upon the throne said, Behold, I make all things new, And he said unto me, Write: For these words are true and faithful. And he said unto me, It is done. I am Alpha and Omega, the beginning and the end, I will give unto him that is athirst of the fountain of the water of life freely. He that overcometh shall inherit all things; and I will be his God, and he shall be my son. but the fearful, and unbelieving, and the abominable, and murderers, and whoremongers, and sorcerers, and idolators, and all liars, shall have their part in the lake which burneth with fire and brimstone; which is the second death.

Revelation 21:4–8

Twelve

Reflection

Guidance from the Light

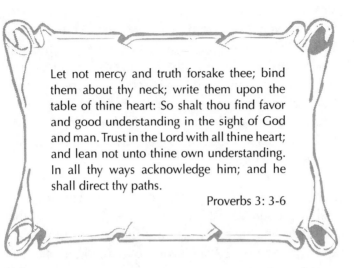

Let not mercy and truth forsake thee; bind them about thy neck; write them upon the table of thine heart: So shalt thou find favor and good understanding in the sight of God and man. Trust in the Lord with all thine heart; and lean not unto thine own understanding. In all thy ways acknowledge him; and he shall direct thy paths.

Proverbs 3: 3-6

These are words to live by. A reflection of one's journey on earth that will help you to make it through the storms in life. We always have a choice. Making the right one may not be so simple at times for some, but know that God loves you and will always be at your side. Always come to God in prayer, and he will lift you up in love and hope and keep you where you need to be. Sometimes all we have to do is use some common sense to deliver ourselves from losing grace. Everyone is not born in a place of comfort and joy, but if life is meant to be, we can change the way we lead our lives, beginning and ending with each step we make in our daily living. Greed has no part in the building blocks of life.

I believe in a holistic approach to living one's life, a fresh start. Every time you wake up from your sleep, you should do unto others as you would have them do unto you. Your life is before you, take time to replenish it every day with the life force of the healing energy that comes from the light of our lord, who died on the cross for our sins so that we may be saved and have everlasting life. Do not just satisfy your physical needs, but meet your spiritual needs also to help you complete your journey. Rejoice in God's words and live a life of assurance that you will be rewarded for your faithfulness. I feel blessed to know that someday my tears will be dried by the hands of the lord.

Reflection can give you a chance to change the way you feel and uplift your spirits in a more positive way that will help you take one day at a time, with more ease and understanding. When you understand the plan that God has for you, you can take the time to realize that all things will be revealed to us and it will be worth the wait, for only the truly faithful will know his blessings in the end. When you think of your life and the direction you are going in, does it show a positive reaction to your fellow man, or do you shy away from anything that is not up to your standards? This is not the direction the lord wants us to go in. We really need to help each other whenever we can.

Jesus was invited to dinner by a woman he knew. He came to her house on several occasions, but he was not dressed in a fashion that was acceptable to her; she thought he was a beggar. One day, he came dressed as himself, and she asked what took him so long to come and have dinner with her and her family. Jesus said he had come before, but each time he did, she turned him away. This story has stuck with me since childhood; when I was a child, a man came to our house asking for food. He was dirty with tattered clothes on. My youngest brother and I were outside playing in the yard when he walked up and asked if we had any food to eat. We went inside and made two bologna sandwiches, as if we were making them for ourselves; we did not tell our mother. We took the sandwiches outside and gave them to the man. He thanked us and walked off, eating the food we had brought him. I never saw him again, and whenever I think of that Bible story, I wonder if that could have been Jesus. Now that I am an adult, I know that whatever we do for each other, we do unto Jesus.

Reflecting on my life as a child has reminded me of a time when I was going in the right direction and did not think of life any other way. Now as adult, I analyze my steps to insure that I am on the right track; I wonder how I can stay steadfast with my beliefs, which require prayer just to get through the day. The pressure is on us all from time to time, and prayer can help us to deal with people who are very unhappy in a more positive way; these people want the world to feel their misery and pain because they are afraid and do not have Jesus in their lives. Misery loves company, so this is one visitor you should definitely pray for and not invite to dinner unless you feel strong enough to handle a problem that could swallow you whole.

When you look in the mirror, what do you see? Are you a shell of a person drifting from day to day, waiting on the grand moment of bliss to slap you in the face? Stop waiting; just be prepared, because Jesus is coming back, and you should not be caught looking at a shell in the mirror. You must be a vibrant person who knows God loves you and will take all your worries away. Having a dream that is tangible in life is what will keep you focused on the most important thing in this world; it will show you a reflection of what you should be doing with the life God gave you. Your reflection shows who you really are and what you reflect to others. What you do with the life given you is your choice, so choose a life that you can reflect on as a journey of mind and soul that has helped you to grow in this world, not remain stagnant.

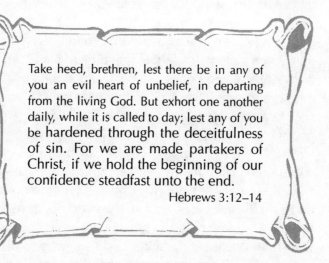

Take heed, brethren, lest there be in any of you an evil heart of unbelief, in departing from the living God. But exhort one another daily, while it is called to day; lest any of you be hardened through the deceitfulness of sin. For we are made partakers of Christ, if we hold the beginning of our confidence steadfast unto the end.

Hebrews 3:12–14

Thirteen

Meditative Visions

These pictures will help you to keep the faith on your journey of hope and redemption.

Faith is the substance of things hoped for, the
evidence of things not seen.

Hebrews 11:1

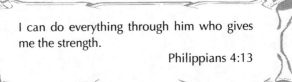

I can do everything through him who gives me the strength.

Philippians 4:13

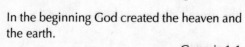

In the beginning God created the heaven and the earth.

Genesis 1:1

And, behold, I came quickly; and my reward is with me, to give every man according as his work shall be.

Revelation 22:12

He that saith he is in the light, and hateth his brother, is in darkness even until now.

1 John 2:9

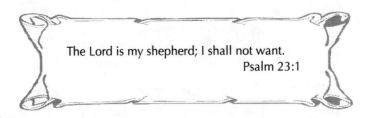

The Lord is my shepherd; I shall not want.
Psalm 23:1

For the Lord giveth wisdom: out of his mouth
cometh knowledge and understanding.

Proverbs 2:6

Remember not the sins of my youth, nor my transgressions: according
To thy mercy remember thou me for thy goodness' sake, O Lord.

Psalm 25:7

Therefore the redeemed of the Lord shall return, and come with singing unto Zion; and everlasting joy shall be upon their head: They shall obtain gladness and joy; and sorrow and mourning shall flee away.

Isaiah 51:11

Wherefore gird up the loins of your mind, be sober, and hope to the end for the grace that is to be brought unto you at the revelation of Jesus Christ;

1 Peter 1:13

Fourteen

Words of Knowledge
(Scripture)

A clear perception of the truth

These words spake Jesus, and lifted up his eyes to heaven, and said, Father, the hour is come; glorify thy Son, that thy Son also may glorify thee: As thou hast given him power over all flesh, that he should give eternal life to as many as thou hast given him. And this is life eternal, that they might know thee the only true God, and Jesus Christ, whom thou hast sent. I have glorified thee on the earth: I have finished the work which thou gavest me to do. And now, O Father, glorify thou me with thine own self with the glory which I had with thee before the world was. I have manifested thy name unto the men which thou gavest me out of the world: thine they were, and thou gavest them me: and they have kept thy word. Now they have known that all things whatsoever thou hast given me are of thee. For I have given unto them the words which thou gavest me; and they have received them, and have known surely that I came out from thee, and they have believed that thou didst send me.

I pray for them: I pray not for the world, but for them which thou hast given me: for they are thine. And all mine are thine, and thine are mine; and I am glorified in them. And now I am no more in the world, but these are in the world, and I come to thee, Holy Father, keep through thine own name those whom thou hast given me, that they may be one, as we are. While I was with them in the world, I kept them in thy name: those that thou gavest me I have kept, and none of them is lost, but the son of perdition; that the scripture might be fulfilled. And now come I to thee; and these things I speak in the world, that they might have my joy fulfilled in themselves. I have given them thy word; and the world hath hated them, because they are not of the world, even as I am not of the world. I pray not that thou shouldest take them out of the world, but that thou shouldest keep them from the evil.

They are not of the world, even as I am not of the world. Sanctify them through thy truth: thy word is truth. And for their sakes I sanctify myself, that they also might be sanctified through the truth. Neither pray I for these alone, but for them also which shall believe on me through their word; that they all may be one; as thou, Father, art in me. And I in thee, that they also may be one in us; that the world may believe that thou hast sent me. And the glory which thou gavest me I have given them; that they may be one, even as we are one. I in them, and thou in me, that they may be made perfect in one; and that the world may know that thou has sent me, and hast loved them, as thou hast loved me. Father, I will that they also, whom thou hast given me, be with me where I am; that they may behold my glory, which thou hast given me: for thou lovedst me before the foundation of the world. O righteous Father, the world hath not known thee: but I have known thee, and these have known that thou hast sent me. And I have declared unto them thy name, and will declare it: that the love wherewith thou hast loved me may in them, and I in them.

John 17: 1-26

The lord is my light and my salvation; whom shall I fear? The Lord is the strength of my life; of whom shall I be afraid? When the wicked, even mine enemies and my foes, came upon me to eat up my flesh, they stumbled and fell. Though an host should encamp against me, my heart shall not fear: though war should rise against me, in this will I be confident. One thing have I desired of the Lord, that will I seek after; that I may dwell in the house of the Lord all the days of my life, to behold the beauty of the Lord, and to enquire in his temple. For in the time of trouble he shall hide me in his pavilion; in the secret of his tabernacle shall he hide me; he shall set me up upon a rock. And now shall mine head be lifted up above mine enemies round about me: therefore will I offer in his tabernacle sacrifices of joy; I will sing, yea, I will sing praises unto the Lord. Hear, O Lord, when I cry with my voice: have mercy also upon me, and answer me.

When thou saidst, Seek ye my face; my heart said unto thee, thy face, Lord, will I seek. Hide not thy face far from me; put not thy servant away in anger: thou hast been my help; leave me not, neither forsake me, O God of my salvation. When my father and my mother forsake me, then the Lord will take me up. Teach me thy way, O Lord and lead me in a plain path, because of mine enemies. Deliver me not over unto the will of mine enemies; for false witnesses are risen up against me, and such as breathe out cruelty. I had fainted, unless I had believed to see the goodness of the Lord in the land of the living. Wait on the Lord: be of good courage, and he shall strengthen thine heart; wait, I say, on the Lord.

Psalm 27:1–14

Be not thou envious against evil men, neither desire to be with them. For their heart studieth destruction, and their lips talk of mischief. Through wisdom is an house builded; and by understanding it is established: And by knowledge shall the chambers be filled with all precious and pleasant riches. A wise man is strong; yea, a man of knowledge increaseth strength. For by wise counsel thou shalt make thy war: and in multitude of counselors there is safety. Wisdom is too high for a fool; he openeth not his mouth in the gate. He that deviseth to do evil shall be called a mischievous person. The thought of foolishness is sin; and the scorner is an abomination to men. If thou faint in the day of adversity, thy strength is small.

Proverbs 24:1–11

Forasmuch then as Christ hath suffered for us in the flesh, arm yourselves likewise with the same mind: for he that hath suffered in the flesh hath ceased from sin; that he no longer should live the rest of his time in the flesh to lusts of men, but to the will of God. For the time past of our life may suffice us to have wrought the will of Gentiles, when we walked in lasciviousness, lusts, excess of wine, revellings, banqueting, and abominable idolatries: Wherein they think it strange that ye run not with them to the same excess of riot, speaking evil of you: Who shall give account to him that is ready to judge the quick and the dead. For for this cause was the gospel preached also to them that are dead, that they might be judged according to men in the flesh, but live according to God in the spirit. But the end of all things is at hand: be ye therefore sober, and watch unto prayer. And above all things have fervent charity among yourselves: for charity shall cover the multitude of sins.

Use hospitality one to another without grudging. As every man hath received the gift, even so minister the same one to another, as good stewards of the manifold grace of God. If any man speak, let him speak as the oracles of God: if any man minister, let him do it as of the ability which God giveth: that God in all things may be glorified through Jesus Christ, to whom be praise and dominion for ever and ever. Amen. Beloved think it not strange concerning the fiery trial which is to try you, as though some strange things happened unto you: But rejoice, inasmuch as ye are partakers of Christ's sufferings; that, when his glory shall be revealed, ye may be glad also with exceeding joy. If ye be reproached for the name of Christ, happy are ye; for the spirit of glory and of God resteth upon you; on their part he is evil spoken of, but on your part he is glorified. But let none of you suffer as a murderer, or as a thief, or as an evildoer, or as a busybody in other men's matters. Yet if any man suffer as a Christian, let him not be ashamed; but let him glorify God on this behalf.

For the time is come that judgment must begin at the house of God; and if it first begin at us, what shall the end be of them that obey not the gospel of God? And if the righteous scarcely be saved, where shall the ungodly and sinner appear? Wherefore let them that suffer according to the will of God commit the keeping of their souls to him in well doing, as unto a faithful Creator.

1 Peter 4:1–19

Conclusion

Inspirational Food for Thought

1. Be inspired to do your best and life will show you the road to success.

2. Walk a mile in someone's shoes and see the life of another's truths.

3. Be the one who brings the light to share with others in their delight.

4. What you say and how you act can be the way to someone's joy in life.

5. When you lie down to sleep at night, think of the lord who brought you through the day with his light.

Lillie Sandridge-Hill

Journey

I would not try to change
Any faith of yours
Or want to seem as if I
Have all the answers to
Your hopes or fears.

There is so much to learn
In this life . . . .
So many things are tried and true.
The journey I have traveled
May not be good for you.

And so I write these words of wisdom
Of what is love and light to me, to guide
You through the darkest moments, but
Not tell you what to see or believe.

Lillie Sandridge-Hill

I'am but a fallen angel; trying to find my way back home to
My heavenly father, who truly loves me and calls me his own.

Lillie Sandridge-Hill

CPSIA information can be obtained at www.ICGtesting.com
Printed in the USA
LVOW052245290413

331508LV00001B/19/P